The LAKE DISTRICT

The
LAKE DISTRICT

CHANCELLOR
PRESS

frontispiece
The hamlet of Watendlath, framed by pines

First published in 1979 by Hamlyn

Seventh impression 1988

This edition published in 1997 by Chancellor Press,
an imprint of Reed International Books Limited,
Michelin House, 81 Fulham Road, London, SW3 6RB
and Auckland, Melbourne, Singapore and Toronto

ISBN 1 85152 198 4

Printed and bound in China

Introduction

The Lake District lies wholly within the modern county of Cumbria though it used to be partly in Cumberland, Westmorland and Lancashire. It has been defined as the area in a circle of fifteen miles radius centring on the village of Grasmere, but perhaps Dunmail Raise, the summit of the pass between Grasmere and Keswick would make a better centre. Today the boundary of the Lake District National Park, designated as such in 1949, is more usually accepted. Its area is 866 square miles, its population is just under 50,000 and its principal towns are Windermere and Keswick. It rises from sea-level at Ravenglass to England's highest mountain, Scafell Pike (3206 ft), and by common consent includes scenery at least the equal of any in the kingdom. This precious place is so small that it deserves the most careful and devoted conservation to ensure that posterity shall have no cause to blame those who look after it, visit it or live and make their livelihood within it for allowing it to pass away.

The fundamental basis of all scenery lies in the structure of the rocks upon which it is formed, and it is the geology of the Lake District which gives it its varied and dramatic character. To the north Skiddaw is composed of some of the oldest rocks in the world, so old that in spite of their hardness they have become smooth during some 500 million years. To the south the Coniston flags are much younger but softer so that they too are smooth. Between them the Borrowdale volcanics composed of lava and ash, so highly compressed that they have become slaty in nature, give rise to the rugged silhouette of the Langdale Pikes and the sound rock faces of Great Gable, beloved of the climbers.

This dome, or at least the major part of it, sank beneath the seas and rose again on various occasions. Layers, first of Carboniferous Limestone, then of the Coal Measures and finally of red sandstone were deposited over the older rocks. When the area was later uplifted again these newer deposits were gradually worn away from the centre and now occur as a fringe round the edge. The limestone outcrops on Kendal Fell and near Penrith. (Measures are now being taken to restrict the removal of 'Westmorland limestone' for rock gardens.) The coal outcrops on the west coast, and the mining operations have extended miles out under the sea. The sandstone gives rise to St Bees Head, the only cliffs along Cumbria's western shore line, and to the fertile valley of the River Eden which flows northwards along the eastern side of the Lake District and so through Carlisle to the quiet Solway Firth which separates Cumbria from Scotland. This outer fringe, though not technically within the Lake District, still includes some remarkable and lovely countryside. Sporadically amongst these rocks the liquid magma of the earth's core forced its way upwards and after countless years has solidified into the granite which is still quarried on Shap, and used to be worked in Eskdale too. The miniature railway, now a tourist attraction familiarly known as the 'Ratty', was built to carry iron ore from Boot in Eskdale. Later it was used to transport this granite.

By comparison with geological time the effect of climate is recent. There have been several Ice Ages – indeed we may now be living in a warm gap between two of them – and the most recent ended about 15,000 years ago. The scars on the rock summit of Bow Fell bear witness to the deep covering of ice which once engulfed the mountain tops. This ice cap slid down the rock slopes, steepening them as it plucked and ground them, gouging out the corrie lakes such as Styhead Tarn below Green Gable, or Angle Tarn north of Bow Fell. Then the glaciers flowed outwards down river valleys which already existed from a previous age, cutting away at their flanks to give the typical U-section of Langdale or Borrowdale. As they went the glaciers shaved off the jutting spurs of the valley sides, whose truncated stumps are to be seen on the south face of Blencathra, east of Keswick, and left the hanging valleys whose foaming white becks now cascade down the steep flanks of the major dales. It was the glaciers which carved out the depressions now occupied by the lakes. The beds of some of them, Windermere and Wastwater for example, are well below sea-level, so it would be impossible to drain them even if their lower ends were not choked and held up by moraines deposited by the retreating glaciers as a warmer climate followed the Ice Age.

It is sad that the current climate of the Lake District has earned for it such an adverse reputation. The rainfall is high and heavy, but as a result of this heaviness the total hours of rainfall are little more than in other parts of Britain. The actual rainfall round the fringe of the fells may be from 40 to 60 inches in a year, but in the heart of the area it may be more than double this amount, varying greatly within a few miles. Not for nothing is the appropriately named Raingauge Cottage, at Seathwaite in the head of Borrowdale, said to be the wettest inhabited place in England. The visitor who relishes the brimming lake, the bubbling torrent, the green field or the deep woodland knows well that without its rainfall the Lake District would not be the place which attracted Wordsworth and still draws people, not only from the rest of Britain but from the world over.

Long after the retreat of the ice, man came to this part of the world. Stone Age man chipped axeheads in Great Langdale and in many other places among the fells where the rock texture was suitable. It must have been a major industry, for its products have been identified as far south as the Thames valley. These axes first put into the hand of man a tool which enabled him to clear the primeval forest and thus to alter the scenery. About 5000 years ago, and then mainly round the fringes of the central massif, man began to grow crops where the land had previously been deep under alder scrub and oak woods. One may speculate whether the introduction of 'newfangled' bronze destroyed the stone axe industry, as man-made fibre now threatens wool, but it seems that the great stone circles such as Castlerigg near Keswick were built during the transitional period from stone to bronze.

The age of iron scarcely reached the Lake District before the Romans whose Wall, spanning England against the Picts, stood along the south shore of the Solway and some distance down the coast. Does their fort at Ambleside at the head of Windermere suggest that they used the lake for transport, and does the better-preserved fort at Hardknott at the head of Eskdale indicate that they planned to cross the sea to the Isle of Man and Ireland? Apart from these military works they left little trace upon the Lake District, its place names or its dialect.

The Roman collapse and evacuation was completed by AD 400, and the Celtic Britons who called themselves Cymry, and bequeathed that name to Cumbria, were left to defend themselves, first against the Picts who pressed south from Scotland and then against the Scots, the race that then lived in Ireland. Later, Anglian people, crossing the North Sea, pressed over the Pennines and conquered them. The British King Dunmail, after whom is named Dunmail Raise on the boundary between Westmorland and Cumberland, where the road from Grasmere to Keswick tops the pass, was defeated by King Edmund of Northumbria in AD 945. He is not buried beneath the pile of stones on top of the Raise, as legend has it, but died in Rome, some years after the battle. The Anglian people were agriculturists and brought with them a new instrument, the heavy ox-drawn plough, with which they ploughed the rich soil of the Eden valley and the fringes of the area; but they scarcely penetrated to the heart of the fells.

At the same time, or a little later the Norsemen, rounding Scotland and settling in Ireland and the Isle of Man, crossed the sea to the west coast. It was they who carved the stone crosses – part Christian,

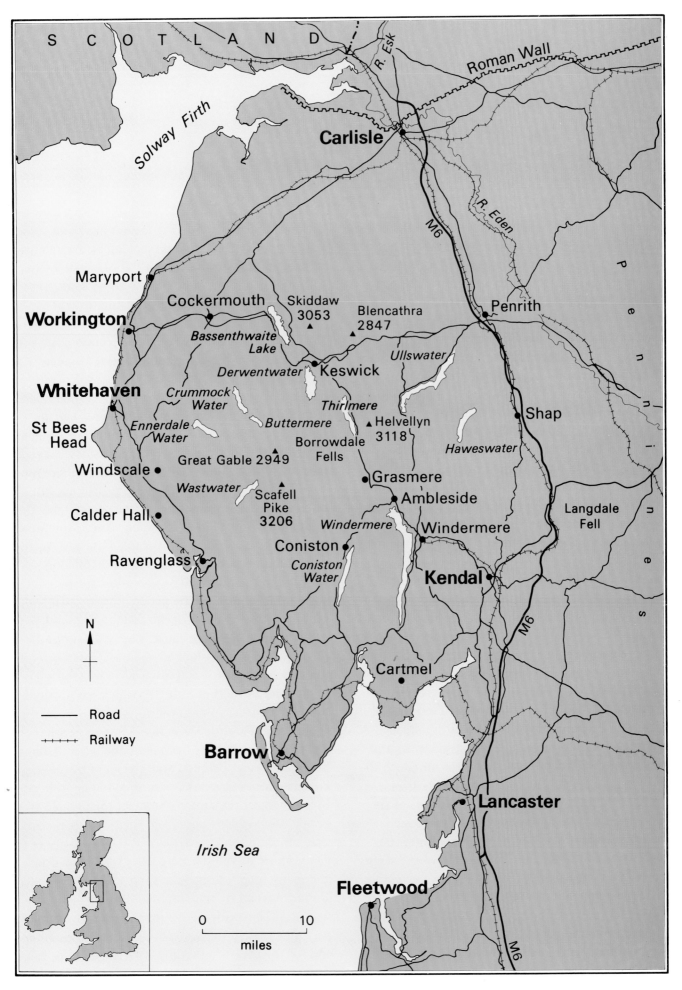

S C O T L A N D

Solway Firth

Roman Wall

R. Esk

Carlisle

M6

R. Eden

Maryport

Cockermouth

Skiddaw
3053 ▲

Blencathra
2847 ▲

Penrith

P

Workington

*Bassenthwaite
Lake*

Ullswater

Derwentwater

Keswick

Whitehaven

*Crummock
Water*

Thirlmere

Shap

St Bees
Head

*Ennerdale
Water*

Buttermere

▲ Helvellyn
3118

Haweswater

e

Windscale ●

Great Gable 2949

Borrowdale
Fells

n

Calder Hall ●

Wastwater

Scafell
Pike
3206 ▲

Grasmere

Ambleside

n

Ravenglass

Windermere

Windermere

Langdale
Fell

Coniston ●

i

*Coniston
Water*

Kendal ●

N

M6

n

Cartmel ●

e

── Road

+++++ Railway

s

Barrow ●

Lancaster

Irish Sea

0   10

Fleetwood

miles

M6

7

part pagan – which still stand in some of the coastal churchyards, the best at Gosforth. It is possible that some of them came not as invaders but as peaceful refugees from their old Norse king who sent his longships against them in the Isle of Man when they set up their own government there. These Norsemen were pastoral in outlook, seeking good grazing for their sheep among the hills reminiscent of their homeland. It was they, more than any other race, who gave the Lake District its dialect and its place names. Their 'thwaite' (a clearing in the woods), now found in Seathwaite, Stonethwaite, Rosthwaite and a hundred other -thwaites, bears witness to their labours; their originals of our fell, tarn, dale, beck and force (waterfall) can still be seen on modern maps of Norway or, indeed, of Iceland. The Anglians and the Norsemen between them established the pattern of Lake District settlement.

Their work and life were too remote to be immediately affected by the Conquest, and it was not until the twelfth century that the land was parcelled out mainly amongst the great religious houses. Furness Abbey had the greatest estates, but Carlisle and Cartmel Priories, Calder and St Bees, and even Fountains over in Yorkshire, owned land amongst the fells. These monks were great sheep farmers and no doubt continued the clearance of the primeval forest. It was at about this time that charcoal began to be made for iron smelting: the pitsteads, the level circular platforms on which the charcoal burners built their smouldering fires, may still be seen in the woods, and the remains of their bloomeries where the smelting took place are frequently identified. So the gradual clearance of the forests continued, and the pattern of the scenery as we know it today began to emerge.

Times remained troublous, and today the pele towers serve to remind us of the border raiders who came from the north to drive off cattle and sheep. These square thick-walled buildings, in which both stock and people could shelter, are sometimes seen as ruins beside still existing farm houses and sometimes as well preserved castles such as Sizergh south of Kendal, now in the care of the National Trust.

Iron was not the only mineral to be worked. Copper on the Old Man of Coniston, lead at Greenside above Glenridding and wad (graphite) in the head of Borrowdale have all left mining scars on the fell sides. The lead mining ceased as recently as 1962, and the pencil industry in Keswick persists to this day, though its raw materials no longer come from Borrowdale. But slate quarrying has made a far greater impact than any other mineral. Almost wherever the rock possessed the necessary characteristic of splitting along flat cleavage lines, there men have worked it, sometimes as open quarries, but often by driving tunnels below the original working in pursuit of the vein of workable slate. The tunnels enabled the material, both useable slate and waste, to be brought out on wheels rather than having to be lifted to the quarry lip. Now the industry concentrates more on the production of sawn and polished slabs of slate for the facing of buildings, rather than on roofing slates. The roads up to the quarries, even when long abandoned, often provide the walker with an easy approach towards the fell tops.

Forestry is another industry which has affected the lake scenery, sometimes improving it, sometimes the reverse. Records show that when the Earl of Derwentwater lost his head after the '45 Rebellion his estates were forfeited and given to Greenwich Hospital who carried out extensive felling, followed by methodical replanting. Some of the fine old trees beside the lake may date from this time. It is said that a million trees were planted by the owner of the Claife shore of Windermere in 1787. These woods, and many others along lake shores and elsewhere, are now owned by the National Trust which manages them with an eye for their beauty, both the part they play in the scenery as viewed from outside, and for the pleasure that big well-grown trees can give to those who walk amongst them.

The effect of State Forestry, started after World War I, has been less happy. The policy was directed towards the rapid production of coniferous timber, and much of the planting, notably on the slopes of Skiddaw, was carried out in geometric patterns which ill-accord with the shape of the land. Only now, as the original plantations begin to be harvested are their harsh edges being softened and moulded into more sympathetic outlines.

Trees in the Lake District have not suffered at the hands of modern agriculture as they have elsewhere in Britain where the eradication of hedgerows has been so disastrous. This is partly because Lakeland fields are separated by stone walls, not hedges, but mainly because the agriculture is based not upon the plough but upon natural grassland. Indeed, were it not for the grazing sheep much of the lower land would quickly revert to scrub and woodland, the condition in which our early ancestors found it.

It is perfectly true to say that the scenery and character of this region owe more to the mountain sheep than any other single influence. The Herdwick sheep is rightly described as indigenous because its ancestry has never been traced to any other type. Legends of its introduction by the Armada from Spain or by the Vikings from Norway are not borne out by any affinity to the breeds of sheep in those countries, or even in Iceland. Herdwick lambs are born black or at least dark-coloured, and as they mature they become paler. It has thus been possible, by sorting the clipped fleeces according to age, and spinning the age groups separately, to produce a patterned tweed of natural coloured wools without resort to the dye tub. Herdwicks have two characteristics which fit them for this region. They have a remarkable ability to foretell the weather and they drop to low ground, often before mere mortals have begun to think of snow. If they are overblown by snow they can survive for long periods beneath it. Stories are told of sheepdogs sniffing at a long-lying drift from which a farmer has dug sheep lost for as long as six weeks. Poor things, they emerge from their ordeal quite naked, having survived by eating their own wool – surviving themselves, and able to bear a lamb a few weeks later. Their other characteristic is their determination to stick to the part of the fell which they regard as their own. A lamb born in the flat fields of the valley bottom, but taken, in early summer to its dam's old haunts, will itself become 'heafed' to that particular spot and will persist there, year after year, taking its successive lambs back to the same place. So the poorer as well as the better grazing is evenly cropped.

As a result of this sense of location – this determination to occupy its own piece of fell land – it has followed that many of the sheep on a farm actually belong to the landlord who lets them with the land and the buildings to his tenant. If the outgoing tenant sold all his sheep when he gave up, the new tenant would be unable to establish a new flock by buying sheep from elsewhere. If he tried they would just walk back across the unfenced fells to the place where they had been first acclimatised. So the outgoing tenant has to hand back to his landlord at least the bulk of his flock (successors, of course, to the originals which he took), and this 'heaf-going' flock is passed on to the incoming farmer. Black-faced sheep such as Swaledales have been introduced to the district, and in favoured places have done well. (Their wool is finer and more valuable than the Herdwick's.) But in the real heart of the fells, say within ten miles of Scafell Pike, it is the pale-faced Herdwick that survives best and makes farming a form of livelihood in these rugged parts.

It has been well said that fell farming is a way of life rather than a way of making good, and the fell farmers without whom the fell sheep would not exist, are a hard-working hardy breed, well heafed, like their sheep, to the area where they belong. For a month each year at lambing time they work eighteen hours a day(no overtime payments for them). They and their equally hardy dogs know every yard of their fell, and they know their sheep. A real Herdwick, for such is the name applied to the farmer as well as to his sheep, will recognise every individual in a flock of more than a thousand. His land is not sufficiently fertile to fatten his sheep for market, so he must perforce sell them as 'stores' for his lowland counterpart to fatten. Notoriously successive governments, in pursuance of a cheap food policy, have subsidised the end product – fat lamb. But too little of this subsidy has found its way back into the pockets of the fell farmer who has produced the store lamb which is eventually fattened for the table.

These hardy men and their wives and families live, often in the remote valley heads, a lonely harsh life divorced from the so-called amenities of civilisation. Their farmhouse, successor perhaps to some wooden and thatched building first erected by their Norse forebears, is of whitewashed stone with a slate roof. Each year the place-proud family applies one more coat of whitewash, traditionally mixed of lime and tallow with a little of the blue-bag to brighten it. Today most of them have electricity and hot water, but it is only recently that these conveniences have reached all areas. Their farm buildings are stone faced. They appear to be built without mortar, and indeed many barns are built 'dry', like the field walls which stand so miraculously. But the cow shippons have mortar between the stones, kept back from the face so that one does not see it. Even so, the ventilation of these buildings is so good that tuberculosis, the dreaded scourge of the lowland cattle farmer, is often unknown here.

The field walls, so characteristic of the floors and flanks of the dales, are in fact built without mortar, sometimes from quarried slaty stones but often from rounded beck cobbles. A wall consists of two outer faces and a core into which all the smaller stones are packed. The two faces are tied together by lines of 'throughs', big flat stones which may often be seen projecting in rows on each side of a wall, or for that matter, from the gable end of a barn. The origins of some walls are lost in time, but the majority of them were built in the eighteenth and early nineteenth centuries at the time of the Enclosure Awards which allotted parts of the common land to be taken in by the various farms in the valley. To this day many of the large enclosures on the flanks of the valley are called allotments or intakes, indicating their origin. Naturally land allotted to a freeholder was useless to him until he had walled it round to keep his own stock in and his neighbour's stock out. The farmers of today are still perfectly capable of building these stone walls. Hard weather, particularly driven snow which expands when it thaws and refreezes, causes many a wall gap which is accepted philosophically and repaired by the farmer. It is the wall gaps made by thoughtless hikers, aiming straight across country towards their goal, which cause such fury in the farmer and engender an antagonism between him who does so such to preserve the district and those who come to enjoy it.

After agriculture the next largest industry of the Lake District is undoubtedly tourism. Even before the days of Wordsworth, who wrote a famous guide to the lakes, visitors were beginning to arrive. A diarist of 1769 who was not brave enough to go beyond Grange-in-Borrowdale wrote ecstatically that 'not a single red tile, no gentleman's glaring house or garden walls break in upon the repose'. The railway reached Windermere in 1847 and Coniston and Keswick in 1865 (the two latter lines are now closed.) Even before the advent of the car it was possible to drive by horse carriage up most of the main valleys and even over many of the passes. The passengers walked up the hills! Now not only is there a daily influx of cars from the south and east, but the inhabitants of the holiday villages are outnumbered many times by the tourists who lodge amongst them throughout the summer. The hospitality of lakeland is justifiably famous, and the relationship between the tourists and those who serve them is almost always a happy one. There are complaints amongst residents that in some villages almost all the shops are selling gifts and postcards, and it is hard to come by an ordinary village shop. There are also complaints, especially from young newly-married couples, that every house on the market is sold to 'off-comers' at prices that local wages can never enable them to afford. There is, of course, plenty of summer work for the womenfolk in the catering trade, and it is certain that, financially speaking, the Lake District would be severely impoverished without its visitors.

This may be the right place to pause and try to assess the essential quality of Lake District scenery that differentiates it from the much higher mountains of the Alps or the more extensive Highlands of Scotland, and inspires and retains such devotion from so many who visit it, often again and again. Perhaps the scale of the scenery is its most particular attribute. Although man has overcome his eighteenth-century horror of the beetling cliff and the dreadful chasm, and although most visitors come to the country in order to 'get away from it all', man still enjoys the feeling that he is in touch with humanity, and he may feel puny and uncomfortable amid mountains that overawe him. In the Lake District the scale of man's activities is just right: he has come to terms with nature rather than taming it. The farmer and his sheep use the whole of the country, but have not imposed themselves on it; they have neither oppressed nor possessed it. The farmsteads and the pattern of field walls bear a kindly relationship to the fells above, even though they often appear to be higher than they really are. The walker on the tops can usually look down on to a ribbon of occupied valley bottom to remind him that he is not in a complete wilderness.

Apart from the scenery and just looking at it, perhaps sketching it or photographing it, the visitor enjoys it in many different ways. Climbing is the classic sport: few British climbers who have attempted Everest have not trained in Langdale or the head of Wasdale. (Sherpa Tien Singhe came *after* his conquest, but was impressed.) But for every climber there are a hundred walkers, most of them aiming for a chosen summit or making a passage from one valley to another. All but a tiny fraction of them accomplish what they have planned, but just a few, some through stupidity but some because of genuine accident, hurt themselves or get lost. It is then that the mountain rescue teams go into well planned and organised action. They are all volunteers, the equivalent of lifeboat men, who give devoted service. When there is genuine need of their help, then they are proud to serve. It is when a walker fails to mention a change of plan, his friends report him missing, and the searchers spend cold weary hours on the fells, perhaps sacrificing their wages to do so, while all the time the 'missing' walker is snug in bed – it is then that the rescue teams get angry.

The lakes themselves provide recreation of a different kind. Sailing becomes increasingly popular, with clubs on several of the larger lakes. The white or coloured sails make a happy addition to the scene, perhaps because they are silent and therefore do not disturb the tranquility. Not so the fast motorboat, often with a water skier towing behind it. Recent bye-laws are banishing them from all the lakes except Windermere where, at times, the hurly-burly is intolerable. Fishing is popular, though the acid nature of the water with its shortage of freshwater shrimps is not conducive to large specimens. There are two interesting kinds of fish to be found in the lakes: in the deepest of them char, a relic of the Ice Age and a relative of the trout, are caught on deep-trolled lines from slow rowingboats. In olden times potted char, in pretty pots, were regularly sent to

Great Gable, Kirk Fell and Piers Gill
from Lingmell Col.

London. The other strange fish is the schelly, a fresh
water relative of the herring, seldom caught, for its
diet is minuscule, but sometimes seen, washed up
and dying, on the shores of Ullswater. Steamers and
launches carry literally millions of trippers on
Windermere, Ullswater and Derwentwater. Recent
enterprise by the National Trust is restoring
Gondola, an iron boat dating from 1859 which will
ply again on Coniston Water after years of neglect.

There are also village sports and sheepdog trials
to while away an afternoon. Though sheepdog trials
may be seen in many hilly parts of Britain, the
Cumbrian style of wrestling, which is a feature of
the village sports, is unique. So is the sport of fell
racing: from the arena the competitors scale the
local high spot and make the return, not checking
their steep descent, but driving themselves down-
wards with their full strength. It is significant that
most of the successful fell runners are fell farmers
during their working lives.

Hound trailing, too, is a purely local sport. The
dogs, with the blood of greyhounds as well as
foxhounds in their ancestry, follow the trail of a
drag soaked in aniseed. As each dog comes in sight
of the finish its owner breaks into a stream of holloas
to encourage its final sprint. Always – even for the
last arrival – there is a tasty morsel for a reward.
Many stories are told of the chicanery of competitors,
of fresh dogs released halfway round the course, of
false trails laid into some outlying barn where all
but the favoured dog are given copious drafts of
water to slow them down when they are all released
again. Some of these stories are true!

There are some who say that it is no longer
possible to find solitude at the Lakes. True, if you
visit Tarn Hows on a Sunday afternoon in spring or
if you walk up the head of Borrowdale, beyond
Seathwaite, on any fine summer day you will be
with other people; but turn a couple of hundred
yards to left or right off the beaten track and there
you will be alone.

If you go quietly into the woods there are red squirrels still surviving and both roe and red deer; the latter, better fed and better sheltered than their brethren in the bleak Scottish Highlands, are some of the best wild specimens in the Kingdom. There are pine martens in the wilder woods, but they are seldom seen. Foxes abound, and they are a cruel menace at lambing time. In order to keep down their numbers they are hunted throughout the winter by several fell packs of hounds. This hunting is done on foot (the fells are unsuited to horses) and the object is more to destroy vermin than to provide sport. Terriers of the hardy Lakeland breed accompany the hunters and are used to kill foxes which have gone to ground. There is no other way of keeping foxes within reasonable bounds. On the west coast, notably on the cliffs of St Bees Head and amongst the sand dunes north and south of Ravenglass, great quantities of sea birds are protected by various organisations while they breed each year. The golden eagle is re-establishing itself as a breeding species and in spite of egg collectors it has on occasion reared fledglings.

Egg collectors are not the only threat to the Lake District. Far more perturbing is the ever-increasing number of motor vehicles, with the corollary of road widening and road straightening. Now that the road from the motorway at Penrith has been improved to serve the new industries in the west coast towns, heavy lorries have been banned from passing through the heart of the district on the main road from Windermere to Keswick. But this improvement has not reduced the number of tourists' cars at the height of the summer. More car parks help to find space off the roads, but traffic management, perhaps in the form of one-way roads or a 'tidal' traffic system may become necessary in the near future.

To meet increasing demands for water, partly for human consumption and partly for industry both to the south of Cumbria and along its west coast, a number of the lakes have become reservoirs. The water of many of them is so pure that it can be safely drunk without treatment. Thirlmere which was raised by a dam at the end of the last century flows by gravity and quite untreated to the taps of the people of Manchester. The same pure water is squandered there on industrial purposes or for washing the streets! Public access to Thirlmere's shores is still denied. Haweswater was raised by a dam about 1920, and it is now suggested that its height should be greatly increased. Its water is now mixed with water from Windermere and Ullswater, and this is treated before it goes down the pipes. On the western fringe of the area Wastwater supplies the Atomic Works at Windscale, and Crummock Water and Ennerdale Water supply the coastal towns and their industry. Moderate extraction has minimal effect on the natural appearance of a lake, but recent demands for emergency powers and for raising the heights of dams show, all too clearly, that once a lake has been harnessed, it is thereafter subject to increasing demands. When, oh when will society learn that cheapness is not the ultimate criterion? Vast quantities of water flow from the lakes into the sea. It is this which should be brought to supply, recognising that, although beauty and recreation have no monetary value they are still great treasures – treasures which, once destroyed, can never be recovered.

Another threat is the erosion of footpaths. Perfectly well-behaved people, in sufficient numbers, particularly when the ground is wet, wear away the natural turf. Then the rain gets to work on the exposed soil and turns the path into a gully which deepens until the walkers choose a new route and the process starts all over again. This problem is being tackled not only by careful research, but by the many young people who ask if they may do voluntary work for the benefit of the community. The National Trust has been pre-eminent in recruiting and deploying these volunteers.

The Trust is a voluntary body which owns about one-fifth of the area and preserves its properties for posterity. It operates under an enlightened policy which allows great public access so long as the people who come do not spoil what they and their successors want to enjoy, and provided they do not interfere with farming and natural history. Another caring body is the Lake District Special Planning Board, a specialised form of Local Government charged with preserving the scenery and promoting public enjoyment, two objects which are often not easy to reconcile. Like most counties today Cumbria has its Naturalists' Trust, which has about a score of nature reserves, and there is a society called the Friends of the Lake District which campaigns vigorously for the amenities.

So what of the future ten, twenty, fifty years ahead? (Who can see further?) Will the charm of the Lake District perish under increasing pressures? Is humanity today so callous about the future that it will bequeath only ruination to its successors? Or will true wisdom prevail, and thought, imagination, careful planning and much hard work (helped perhaps by the shortage of petrol as world reserves of oil are inevitably exhausted) succeed in keeping it in a condition in which successive generations will be able to enjoy it?

Of one thing we can be tolerably certain – the silhouette of the Langdale Pikes or of Great Gable must have looked much the same as they do now, when our ancestors first began to penetrate amongst them more than 5,000 years ago, and there is no reason why the fells – the enduring mountains – will not look the same 5,000 years into the future.

Cubby Aalaine

Greathall Gill, Wasdale, a volcanic shatterbelt, in eerie contrast to the green valley far below.

From Great End Col the Gables (*below right*) do
not seem too formidable, but in fact Great Gable,
seen here (*below*) across Lingmell Beck in Wasdale,
has some of the most testing climbs in the whole
of the Lake District.

A packhorse bridge in Wasdale Head (*right*),
without parapet so as not to impede the packs the
animals carried.

Windermere, the largest of the lakes, has
enough space to accommodate all tastes, from the
nostalgically old-fashioned steamer to the
breathtaking (and earsplitting) power boat. But for
some a rubber dinghy is the ultimate in excitement,
especially when others look enviously on.

Old houses (*left*) span the street in Hawkshead.
Wordsworth went to the Grammar School here.

At Grasmere Sports *(below)*, in the very centre
of the Lake District, events unique to the area can
be seen. In hound-trailing the animals follow a
trail of aniseed over a ten-mile course round
the fells. Cumberland and Westmorland wrestlers
grunt and sweat under the close scrutiny
of the connoisseurs.

The Guides' Race at Grasmere Sports (*top right*) draws spectators to the top of the fell for a grandstand view. But for most people the lure of the hills, as here in Borrowdale, is in walking and rockclimbing. Each can be hazardous for the careless or irresponsible, but the rescue teams, never far away, are amazingly philosophical about bringing such people to safety.

Much of the farming in Borrowdale, as elsewhere in the Lakes, consists of sheep. Here at Seathwaite, reputedly the wettest inhabited place in the country, the sheep are the local Herdwick breed. Even newly clipped they are hardy enough not only to withstand the climate, but to do well on the rather poor grazing of the fells. The men, too, are a durable breed, self-reliant and quite accustomed, even when well past the prime of life, to spending a long day on the hills tending their animals. Seathwaite was not always given over entirely to agriculture. In places spoil heaps of the old graphite mine can still be seen (*right*), and today forestry also plays a part in the economy. Though tented tourists abound, most of them are probably largely self-sufficient.

Rosthwaite, Borrowdale (*below*).

Seathwaite Farm (*right*). 'In-by' land is vital at lambing time or when heavy snow threatens.

Rocks dropped by melting glaciers or rolled along under great ice sheets litter the valleys of the Lake District. Torrential rainstorms, turning the becks into torrents, add their quota of boulders. This (*below right*) is Stonethwaite.

Autumn at Langstrath Beck in Borrowdale.

On the tops (this is the summit of Pavey Ark,
Langdale Pikes) the wild landscape and the menace
of the weather can seem overwhelming to the timid
walker. But, unlike other, more remote parts of
Britain, the Lake District has a good scattering of
farmsteads, as at Watendlath, so that there are
generally other people not too far off.

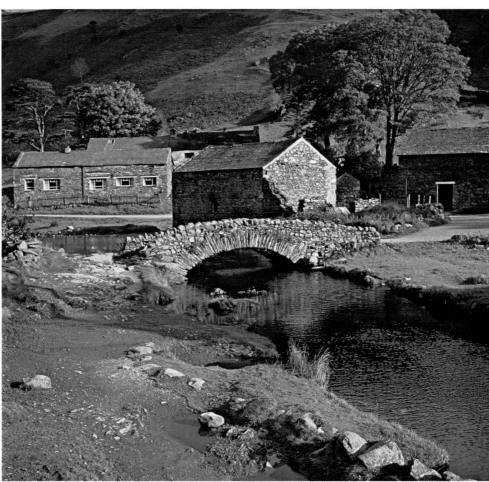

There is a narrow road leading to Watendlath,
but it is much more rewarding to follow one of the
footpaths to the hamlet, particularly one along the
beck. The visitor will then cross this fine packhorse
bridge where the beck flows out of the tarn.
Watendlath was used by Sir Hugh Walpole
as a setting in his Herries saga, a series of four
novels published in the early 1930s – *Rogue Herries,
Judith Paris, The Fortress* and *Vanessa*.

Though the Vale of Rydal Sheepdog Trials
attract visitors from outside the Lake District, it is
of real importance to the local people, for whom
the finer points of a hound or the performance of a
sheepdog are matters of everyday life, rather than
just part of a holiday spectacle.

Langdale Pikes are not the highest fells in the
Lakes, but they are among the most imposing.
Whether seen from a distance across Blea Tarn
(*below*) or from Stickle Tarn under the summit of
Pavey Ark *(right)*, they seem to hold
a brooding mystery.

Prehistoric man found in some of the Lakeland mountains, such as the steep slopes of Pike O' Stickle (*left, furthest pike*), volcanic rocks with a fine hard texture suitable for the making of stone axes for felling trees; a regular industry was established on such a scale that finished tools were 'exported' to the furthest corners of England. These implements were bartered for the necessaries of life, food, clothes, pottery and other kinds of tools, such as bone fishhooks. This extensive trade between specialist craftsmen and the food-producers in Neolithic times was the beginning of the end for self-sufficiency which has only become fashionable again in the last few years.

Ambleside, at the northern end of Windermere,
derives its name from *Hamelsaetr*, the Norse words
meaning *saetr* (summer grazing) of Hamel, the
Norse leader. This tiny cottage (*left*), built over the
water, was originally the whimsical summerhouse
of Ambleside Hall. By contrast, the farmhouse
at Watendlath (*above*) is a real countryman's
house, sturdy, practical, a sure protection against
wind and weather, but proudly whitewashed to
show off the flowers.

This impressive cliff of loose rocks, the Screes (*left*), plunges into Wastwater from a height of 2000 feet.

Storm clouds build up over Tarn Hows, owned by the National Trust. It is an artificial lake made by a dam, which caused three little tarns to merge into one. Indeed, some people still refer to it as the Three Tarns.

Between Ravenglass and Ambleside lies Hardknott Pass, and here the Romans built a fort beside the road they had constructed joining their settlements at these two places. The Romans no doubt were more concerned with establishing a good defensive position for their fort than with finding a place with the best view, but the result is that they achieved both. One wonders whether the ordinary Roman soldier, blowing on his hands in deep midwinter, appreciated his magnificent surroundings.

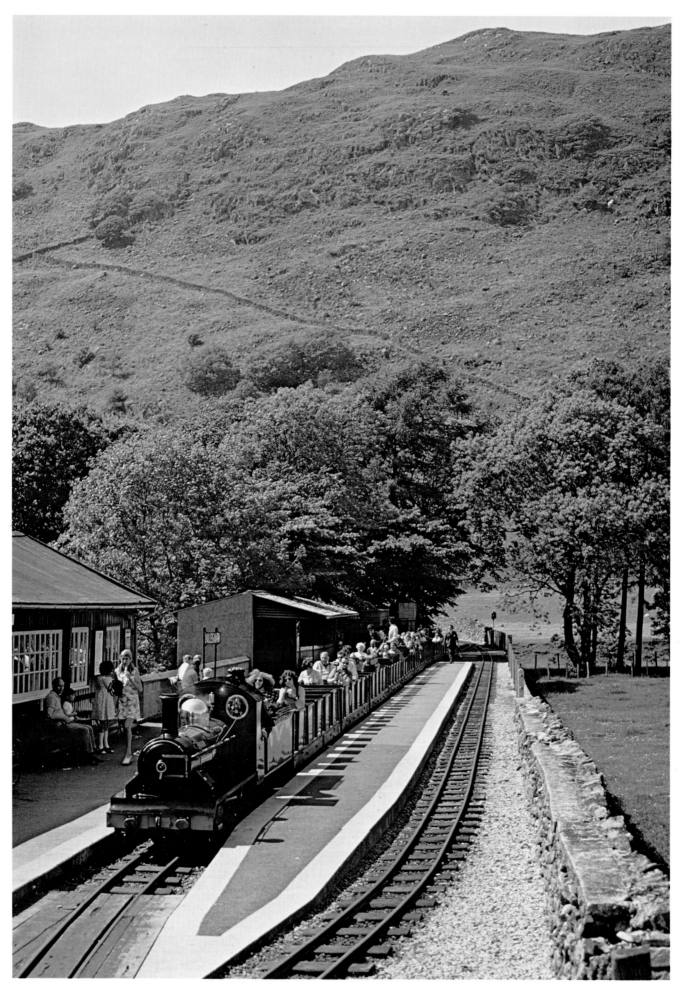

The Ravenglass and Eskdale Railway (*left*), or
'Ratty' as it is familiarly known, was laid in the
1870s to carry ore from the mines at Boot. The
railway is today run by a Preservation Society for
the entertainment of visitors and (can one doubt it?)
for the pleasure of the members of the Society.
It is clearly a matter of pride that the 15in.-gauge
track and rolling stock are kept so immaculate.
Here the *River Irt* has just pulled into
Dalegarth station.

One does not always remember that the Lake
District has a coastline. Whitehaven (*above*) was
once one of the area's major ports, as this view of
the extensive harbour shows, but now has just a
small fishing fleet and some ships carrying
phosphate rock from North Africa for the Marchon
chemical works. Peaceful now, it has had its share of
excitements. In 1788 the American John Paul
Jones impudently attacked the town and got as far
as sailing into the harbour where he damaged some
ships. His example was followed in 1915 by a
U-boat which came and shelled the town for
obscure reasons of its own.

Lest it be thought that the 20th century has
passed the Lake District by, two modern status
symbols, Calder Hall and Sellafield, glitter near the
shore. When Calder Hall (*above*) was opened in
October 1956, it was the world's first full-scale
nuclear power station, a remarkable beating of
swords into ploughshares in the eleven short years
following Hiroshima. Not far away, at Sellafield,
the silver sphere of the reactor coolly hides the
nuclear holocaust within.

Sellafield uses an Advanced Gas-cooled
Reactor which has been in commission since 1962.
Although the reactor drives generators producing
a considerable quantity of electricity, its main
purpose was to prove that the system, and
particularly its slightly enriched fuel, would work
satisfactorily for long periods, which it has now
amply demonstrated. After much controversy, plans
have recently been approved to enlarge the plant,
so that it can process 'Oxide' fuel, including that
brought from Japan.

By way of contrast with the previous few pages,
St Bees Head and Moricambe Bay show nature left
much to her own devices. St Bees Head, with its fine
red sandstone cliffs, is a thronged nesting place
for seabirds, among them fulmars. Just this side of
the headland, Fleswick Bay attracts those who
collect semi-precious stones.

Moricambe Bay, on the other hand, is one of
the loneliest stretches of Cumbrian coast and draws
few creatures but the birds, mainly ducks and
waders. At low tide a vast area of mud flats is
exposed, providing a rich feeding area for
waders, which search out tasty crustaceans such as
the shrimp-like sandhoppers. The pink-footed
goose frequently winters in the bay, while
the rare barnacle goose, wintering nearby,
sometimes visits.

At the seaward end of Moricambe Bay,
Grune Point provides grazing for sheep, but
those that wander on to the salt marshes can be
caught and swept away, when a high tide combines
with a westerly gale. But the Solway Firth has
its attractions. The oystercatchers and other
wading birds find food and to spare along the flat
margin of the Firth. For the riding school the
sands are an awkward mixture of sand and pebbles,
but riders are rewarded with pleasant views of the
Scottish coast across the estuary. In the estuary
itself haaf-net fishing, said to have been introduced
by the Vikings, involves the fishermen standing
in line in the water, the outermost man with the
incoming tide swirling round his shoulders. The
haaf-net is loosely hung on an enormous frame,
some 16ft by 5ft in size, with a large central
handle, like a monstrous shrimping-net, which it
takes great strength and skill to control. Since they
catch the salmon as they enter the estuaries, these
men are none too popular with inland fishermen.

Honister Crag and Honister Pass, here seen
on a cold clear winter day. The road winding up
the valley is alarmingly steep in places, but the view
from the pass is well worth the effort.

Innominate Tarn, on the summit plateau
of Hay Stacks, with Pillar behind. The summit
is a glaciated platform with rock pools, peaty tarns,
hummocks and craggy outcrops.

Erosion caused not by wind and rain, but
by thousands of human feet, is a relatively new
hazard in the English countryside. At Friars Crag,
near Keswick, paths like this one have been
cordonned off for use, while other parts recover.
The International Symbol of Access indicates
suitability for the handicapped, for the National
Trust has created a nature trail for this group
of people.

Newlands (*right*), seen here from Knott Rigg,
was not always so peaceful. In Elizabethan times
German miners, considered the most expert, dug
copper and lead out of the valley.

Sailing Week on Bassenthwaite Lake.

Hunting is a favourite sport in the Lakes.
After all, it is John Peel country, and in 1977
the bi-centenary of his birth was marked with due
ceremony at Caldbeck where he was born and is
buried. The Cumberland Farmers Foxhounds, here
seen arriving at the village, were among the
many who took part in the celebrations. The
Cumberland Farmers is a mounted hunt, unlike the
Blencathra Foxhounds which was John Peel's.
Peel was huntsman for 55 years, while Johnny
Richardson, seen with his pack at a meet, has some
way to go with only 31 years behind him in the
post. Above is Blencathra itself.

Troutbeck Moor and Blencathra (*left*) in
winter's grip.

Buttermere village from Sour Milk Gill (*below*).
Buttermere and Crummock Water, originally one
lake, were eventually divided by material brought
down the hillside by lateral streams. The area
of rich soil so produced, with its heavy cultivation, is
in striking contrast to the barren country around.

Brandy Gill and the Carrock Mine in the
Caldbeck Fells. Lead first attracted miners to the
area, but during the two World Wars it was the
tungsten ores at Carrock Mine that brought the
mining companies here. After a long closure,
the mines are working again, though the deposits
are not large. The whole locality, especially Brandy
Gill, is famous among collectors for the rare
minerals which have been found there.

It is said that the Castlerigg Stone Circle
was used by late Neolithic man as a calendar:
sight-lines at sunrise would give various fixed dates
in the year. Computers have been used to work
out where the stars would have been in 1400 BC
in relation to the stones of this and other such
circles, and lines have been drawn on maps to prove
one theory and to demolish another. The only
certain fact is that the builders chose a superb site: a
platform almost ringed by mountains.

Calf Close Bay, Derwentwater.

Summer visitors would be surprised at the
variety of winter in the Lakes. Snow, mist, cloud
and sun transform the landscape into an ethereal
fantasy, as in this view of Keswick and
Derwentwater from near Millbeck (*above*). A clear
day with bright sunshine on the ice of Derwentwater
and the distant Newlands fells is the other side of
the coin. Derwentwater is always one of the
earliest lakes to freeze.

The quiet beauty of Derwentwater.

The wooded shores of Derwentwater add
greatly to its charm, and it is particularly pleasing
to see areas of natural woodland with native
broad-leaved trees preserved by the National Trust,
when so much of the remoter countryside is under
cultivated conifer forest. Brandelhow was the
first National Trust property in the Lake District.

The small ledges to be seen in the upper
Glenderamackin Valley in the Blencathra range
are the result of a process known as terracing by
needle-ice. At high altitudes in winter packs of ice
crystals form in the soil on steep slopes. Capillary
action draws the water up, and soil particles
and small stones are moved in the process. The
complicated mechanical forces involved produce
little terraces, helped by erosion through
rainwater and sheep-grazing.

Geometrical forestry disturbs the eye.

Hang-gliding at Whittas Park, near Bassenthwaite.

Thousands of fell-walkers follow the track up
Grisedale towards Striding Edge and Helvellyn,
but few are aware of Lanty Tarn, half a mile from
their route, a tiny gem clasped by the trees.

Grisedale Beck, after a heavy snowfall, sparkles
and rings in the crisp morning air.

The High Stile range, seen in winter from
Dale Head (*below*), looks distinctly forbidding. But,
characteristically of the Lakeland mountains,
summer sunshine turns all to smiles and benign
good-humour, as in this view (*below right*) of
High Crag and High Stile from
Gatesgarthdale Beck.

Thin winter sunshine at Dancing Gate, near
Keswick (*top right*).

Mining has for centuries been a major activity in the Lake District. On Honister Pass huge quantities of slate have been removed, leaving spoil heaps, unexpected hollows and abandoned buildings which increase the melancholy appearance of an already bleak landscape. But nearby newer workings are being quarried, much of the slate being exported. The Carrock Mine in Mosedale (*left above*), where tungsten has been produced at intervals since the First World War, is now open again, though here it looks inactive. A busier view of this mine is to be seen on page 60.

Rake Foot (*left*), near Keswick, is one of the
main access points to the fine walk along the crest
of Walla Crag and Falcon Crag, rewarding the
energetic with majestic panoramas over
Derwentwater and Bassenthwaite Lake. Farms in
exposed places often crouch in the shelter of a line
of trees for protection against the prevailing wind.
Farmers, though busy men, are never too occupied
for what is locally known as 'having a crack'.

The River Caldew in Mosedale.

These two pictures represent the ideal of
the summer visitor to the Lake District – sunshine,
fluffy clouds, placid water, a leafy lane and a
distant prospect of shapely fells. Loweswater, with
Grasmoor seen behind, is one of the lesser-known
lakes, which perhaps accounts for the absence
of people, another ideal for most visitors that is not
often fulfilled. The lane is in Mosedale.

Surrounded by wild country, Seatoller (*below left, right*) offers peace and shelter for the traveller.

Low Bridgend Farm, St-Johns-in-the-Vale (*below*), is a very typical Lakeland farmhouse. Nestling under the hills behind, the sturdily built house has been freshly whitewashed, even to the chimney above the slate roof. St Johns Beck (*left*) flows gently through the vale, joining three other waterways, Greta, Glenderaterra and Glenderamackin just below Blencathra.

The curiously named Cat Bells and Skiddaw from Maiden Moor.

Bewcastle cross is remarkable evidence of a sophisticated culture in this part of Britain in the latter part of the seventh century or the beginning of the eighth. These Anglian crosses also occur at Workington and Irton.

Talkin Tarn (*below*), near Brampton, like so many of the lakes, was gouged out during the Ice Age which left its mark all over the northern half of Britain.

Woodlands near Cotehill (*right*) responding happily to the coming of spring.

The River Gelt (*below right*), in Gelt Woods, carries a raging torrent after heavy hill storms, and has cut a deep gorge on its way to the River Eden.

An altogether calmer River Gelt (*left*) than
on page 89. Graffiti from earlier times are not
unknown: near this spot a Roman Legion carved its
record on a rock in the third century.

Spring beeches (*below left*) by the River Eden.

Nunnery Walks (*below*), a beech-lined track
between Kirkoswald and Armathwaite.

Much of the Eden valley round Armathwaite
has been planted with conifers by the Forestry
Commission (see page 96), but happily many acres
of deciduous woodland remain, such as part of
Coombs Wood (*left*).

The grayling may or may not bite, but
the cold winter wind certainly does, despite thin
sun, many layers of clothing and perhaps
something in a flask.

The River Eden near Armathwaite crosses
a bed of soft sandstone, cutting curious patterns
of pools as it does so. Occasionally it encounters a
harder igneous rock which, resisting the current,
forms a cataract of 'white water' (*below right*)
much loved by intrepid canoeists.

At a fish hatchery on the River Eden (*right*) a
salmon is prepared for stripping.

A light snowfall coats the Forestry Commission
plantation near Armathwaite.

Brougham Castle (*top right*), on the banks of
the Eamont near Penrith, can trace its ancestry back
to a Roman fort (*Brocavum*) close by, via a
series of strongholds beginning in Henry II's time.
Blencow Hall (*below right*) was built as a fortified
house against the Scots marauders in the
fifteenth and sixteenth centuries.

97

98

An August landscape (*left*) near Penrith on
the sandstone ridge.

Penrith, like many border towns, has
narrow streets (some once had gates) with wide
squares, an effective defensive system against
raiders from across the border. A market has been
held here since 1223, when Henry III granted a
charter to 'the Royal Town of Penrith'. Market day
is Tuesday, and traders come with textiles from
Lancashire and Yorkshire.

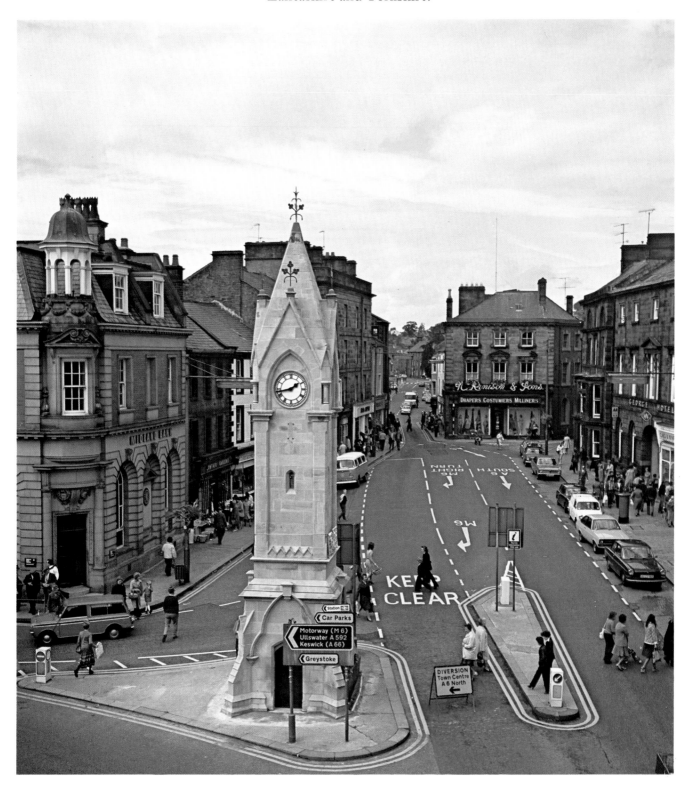

Lowther is one of the great estates of the
Lake District. Little remains of the family home
of the Lowthers, who now live in Askham Hall
across the valley. But in former times royalty in the
person of Mary Queen of Scots was entertained
here, and before the First World War the Kaiser
came to Lowther. In the eighteenth century
James Lowther, known as 'Wicked Jimmy', was

created Earl of Lonsdale, but probably the
best-known member of the family was the 5th Earl,
the famous Yellow Earl, after whom boxing's
Lonsdale Belt is named. This sporting connection
is still maintained in the Lowther
Horse Driving Trials.

It is pleasant that royal links, too, are kept
up, with the presence at these Trials of the Duke of
Edinburgh, seen here in 1973 navigating (it might
almost be said) the River Lowther at Whale
Bridge during the marathon.

During the rest of the year, the main
attraction for visitors is the Lowther Wildlife Park,
with its fine herd of red deer.

Sunbiggin Tarn and its gullery.

Ponies graze undisturbed near Sunbiggin
Tarn, also to be seen on the previous pages, a small
lonely stretch of water on a limestone moor just
south of Appleby. Its remoteness restricts the
number of human visitors and makes it an
ideal breeding place for birds.

The gullery thus provides swarms of birds
to follow the plough on the farmland below
the moor, as here at Scar-side Farm near Orton.
Orton is situated on part of the limestone which
surrounds the central volcanic massif of the
Lake District, and its soil is more fertile
than that of the dale heads.

Old customs are apt to live long in the
Lake District, and the ceremony of rushbearing
at the village of Warcop is still performed each year
on the nearest Saturday to St Peter's Day. The
youngest ladies of the community parade with
crowns of flowers, while the boys follow with
rushes made into crosses. There are banners, music,
a service in the church, refreshments in the village
hall and cheerfulness everywhere. At Appleby Fair,
too, tradition lingers, with gypsies bringing their
horses to town for others to admire.

Clapper Bridge, Waterhouses.

In the twelfth century Sir Hugh de Morville
and his sister Maud each inherited one of the twin
hamlets of Meaburn. Hugh was implicated in the
murder of Becket, and his land, ironically in view of
the King's involvement, was forfeited to the Crown
as punishment. This village became, and remains,
King's Meaburn, while the other was known as
Maud's Meaburn, now corrupted to 'Maulds'.

The River Lyvennet, which runs through
Maulds Meaburn, is a limestone stream containing
considerable numbers of crayfish. It is a
tributary of the River Eden. The river and the
gentle slope behind Maulds Meaburn contrast
strangely with High Cup Nick, only a few
miles away.

High Cup Nick, a dramatic amphitheatre of
igneous rock (the Great Whin Sill) is in the
Pennines above Dufton. The same rock juts up out
of the landscape all over northern England, from
the Farne Islands on the east coast to
Hadrian's Wall, where its outcrops form part
of the defences.

A rainbow at Aira Force.

Ullswater and Glenridding from Birkhouse Moor.

Haweswater and Riggindale from the old
'Corpse Road' on Mardale Common. Until about
1728 there was no consecrated burial ground at
Mardale, so corpses in their coffins were taken on
horseback or on sledges across Swindale Fell
to Shap, ten miles away. Even after Mardale got its
own graveyard the tradition of burial at Shap
was strong enough to make the inhabitants spurn
the new amenity. Haweswater is a Manchester
reservoir, and the light margin is an
indicator of consumption.

Dacre Castle, a medieval pele tower. Its
peaceful aspect contradicts its turbulent history.
The castle is probably on the spot where
Aethelston, the Saxon king, received the
submission of all the kings of the island in
AD 926, although it was not built until over
400 years later.

A fine old building at Hartsop, near Patterdale, apparently (but not in fact) made without mortar, like a dry-stone wall. There is a spinning gallery over the front door.

One of the most famous British lead mines,
the Greenside Mine near Glenridding, closed in
1962. But the buildings are now used by a
number of bodies, including the Youth Hostel
Association and local authorities, as an
outdoor activities centre.

The motor yacht *Raven* at Howtown, Ullswater.
Built by Rutherglens of Glasgow, she was launched
in 1889. She was converted from steam to diesel
and can now reach a speed of 16 knots.

Waterskiing on Ullswater. Following a
public enquiry, a proposal to ban waterskiing on
this lake was upheld by the Minister, subject to a
five-year period of grace to allow the skiers to
find another venue.

Dusk transforms familiar views of Ullswater.

A storm over Ullswater (*right*) has pushed the
lake into the trees on the shoreline.

Ullswater from Martindale Hause, near
Howtown. Howtown, approached by an extremely
narrow road where traffic is often brought
to a standstill, is nevertheless one of the most
popular places for boating.

Park Brow, above Ullswater.

Ullswater – idyllic Lakeland, as the visitor
likes to remember it.

Acknowledgments

The photographers were responsible for the
illustrations as follows:

W. F. Davidson: pages 12–13, 16–17, 18, 19 (bottom), 21
(bottom), 22, 24, 26 (bottom), 27, 28, 29 (both), 30–31, 32, 33,
34, 35 (both), 36, 37, 41 (top), 46, 47, 48 (top), 49 (both), 50,
51, 53, 54–55, 57, 58, 59, 60, 61, 62–63, 65, 66, 67, 68, 69,
70, 71 (left), 72, 73, 74, 75 (bottom), 76 (bottom), 77, 78,
80–81, 82, 84 (top), 85 (bottom), 86–87, 88 (both), 89 (both),
90 (both), 91, 92, 93, 94, 95 (bottom), 96, 97 (both), 98 (both),
99, 102–103, 104, 105, 107, 108, 109, 110, 111, 112, 113, 114,
115, 120, 121, 122, 124–125, 126.

R. Thomlinson: frontispiece and pages 19 (top), 20 (top),
21 (top), 23 (both), 25 (both), 26 (top), 38, 39, 40, 41 (bottom),
42, 43, 44, 45, 48(bottom), 52, 56 (both) 64, 66 (top) 71 (right),
75 (top), 76 (top), 79, 83, 84 (bottom), 85 (top), 95 (top), 100,
101, 106 (both), 116, 117, 118, 119, 123, 127.